Trusting God Series Book one

Powerful Prayers to Protect & Bless your Family

Empower Your Family with God's Word

Lynda D. Brown

I dedicate this book to my mother and father, Leon and Helen R. White, who departed this earth a few years ago. They're now in Heaven looking down on us with the rest of the saints cheering us on as we finish our race.

ISBN: 978-0-9850913-5-4

Table of Contents:

Introduction

"Be alert and of sober mind. Your enemy the devil prowls around like a roaring lion looking for some-one to devour." 1 Peter 5:8 (NIV)

Movie Theater and mall shootings, school shoot-ings, work place mas-sacres, missing college students, child abuse, elder abuse, animal abuse, etc. Our loved ones head off to work, only to be shot or killed by a co-worker. Some parents send children off to school, and end up devastated when their child never returns home. Teens hanging out with friends at the mall can end up hurt or killed. Thousands of senior citizens living in nursing homes are sexually abused and neglected regularly.   Parents, who leave their children home with relatives or day care centers, can sometime be playing Russian roulette with their children's lives.

We're living in very turbulent times

Everyone is running scared, and that's exactly what the enemy wants: He wants you to be afraid.

According to the Word of God, Christians should not be afraid. He gave us **authority and dominion** over everything on Earth and nothing should be happening down here on Earth without our say so! "Look, I have given you authority over all the power of the enemy and you can walk among snakes and scorpions and crush them. Nothing will injure you." (Luke 10:19 NIV)

A few years ago, I made the decision to pray every morning and spend some quality time alone with God. However, I found myself struggling with what to say. I finally broke down and asked the Holy Spirit to help me, and boy did He ever! The Holy Spirit began teaching me about spiritual warfare, praying in the spirit and intercessory prayer. In other words, He taught me how to **strategically** pray.

We're at war with a very old and crafty enemy, but always remember 1 John 4:4 "**Ye are of God, little children, and have overcome them, because greater is He that is in you than he that is in the world.**" Once I made the commitment to transform my way of thinking by **renewing my mind** with the word of God, I've been blessed with **revelation knowledge**, and you need revelation knowledge to defeat the enemy. Intellectual knowledge is not going to work. Man is neither wise enough nor strong enough to defeat the devil by himself. If you don't believe me, grab your Bible and flip over to Acts 19: 11-17. God was working some mighty miracles through Paul. After seeing people get delivered from evil spirits by Paul, some of the Jewish exorcists decided to cast out spirits too. Here's what happened:

"Now God worked unusual miracles by the

hands of Paul, so that even handkerchiefs or aprons were brought from his body to the sick, and the diseases left them and the evil spirits went out of them. Then some of the itinerant Jewish exorcists took it upon themselves to call the name of the Lord Jesus over those who had evil spirits, saying, 'We exorcise you by the Jesus whom Paul preaches.' Also there were seven sons of Sceva, a Jewish chief priest, who did so. And the evil spirit answered and said, 'Jesus I know, and Paul I know; but who are you?' Then the man in whom the evil spirit was leaped on them, overpowered them, and prevailed against them so that they fled out of that house naked and wound- ed. This became known both to all Jews and Greeks dwelling in Ephesus; and fear fell on them all, and the name of the Lord Jesus was magnified."

How do you get revelation knowledge? Here's what the scriptures say in Romans 12:2 from the Message Bible: "So here's what I want you to do, God help-ing you: Take your everyday, ordinary life—your sleeping, eating, going-to-work, and walking-around life—and place it before God as an offering. Embrac-ing what God does for you is the best thing you can do for him. Don't become so well-adjusted to your culture that you fit into it without even thinking. In- stead, fix your attention on God. You'll be changed from the inside out. Readily recognize what he wants from you, and quickly respond to it. Unlike the cul- ture around you, always dragging you down to its level of immaturity, God brings the best out of you, develops well-formed maturity in you."

After meditating on everything the Lord had shown me, He then led me to Hosea 4:6 "My people perish from lack of knowledge." I had read this text in the Bible before, but it wasn't until I had revelation knowledge that I realized the Lord was referring to Christians and not the world in general. He told me that many Christians are ignorant about the things that can hurt them spiritually; he even used my life as an example. "You have loved me since you heard about Me in Sunday school when you were a little girl. You grew up in a church that you loved and had a pastor that you loved and respected, however, when you turned 16, you didn't see any of my promises being fulfilled in your life, so you left me, and turned to astrol- ogy and witchcraft to try and change your life. Many Christians attend church, pay tithes, and read about the promises I have set before them, however, the enemy, does not want to see Christians living the abundant life my son died on the cross for them to have. When they begin to believe the promises and reach for the abundant life I have for them, the en- emy sends trials and tribulations against them to in- timidate and put fear in their hearts. He very easily convinces them to settle for comfortable, ordinary lives. Because they listen to the lies of the enemy, many miss out on the wonderful life I have for them. They refuse to really trust and believe in me. So many Christians, Lynda, do what you did; they begin to seek answers in horoscopes and astrology books; or the services of fortunetellers, numerologist, and other things that are not of Me, when they become sick and tired of the emptiness of their lives."

I've studied and listened to those who real- ly believe God's word and trust Him, and now my dreams have become a reality because I took the time to renew my mind with God's Word. Remem- ber, we have an enemy that does not want us to discover who we are. His mission is to kill, steal and destroy us by any means necessary before we do.

The Lord instructed me to share this testimony with you: In September 2009, I finally finished the first draft of my fiction novel Invisible Enemies, a supernatural thriller based on the Book of Job. A week later, I was on my way to work when out of nowhere, this white car came at me like a missile! I was driving a 2001 Dodge Stratus at the time, and when that car hit me, my little car sailed over the empty right lane, and slammed into a building! Both my airbags exploded, causing me to pass out. When I came to, I saw the employees rushing out of the building I hit, running towards me. However, when they saw the condition of my car, one of the work- ers ran back inside to call 911. When I looked in my rearview mirror and saw the fire department and paramedics arriving, I began to breathe a sigh of re- lief. However, they suddenly stopped and ran back towards their trucks. Panicking, I struggled to get out of my seat belt, and that's when I looked down and saw my hand and arm. My right hand was swol- len twice its size and bleeding, and my left arm was cut and required stitches to close the wound on it. Thank God I had been saying this prayer of protec- tion! Here's the car below:

Growing up in church, I had always heard the Word, and a few times I've read the Word, from Genesis to Revelation. However, it wasn't until I began to really believe the Word and trust the Word of God that I became a doer of the Word, and stepped out on faith and started my own publishing company. Both my books have appeared on Amazon's Best Sellers List. Now that's faith!

Once the enemy realized I had discovered who I was in Christ and what my purpose was here on earth, he had every intention of trying to scare me off by orchestrating a horrific car accident that totally destroyed my car, and severely injured my right hand, which of course is my writing/typing hand! He couldn't kill me because I'm on an assignment from God. I will finish the course the Lord set for me! I'm having the time of my life! Yes, I'm having some attacks and setbacks, but I've learned how to fight back with the tools and the weapons the Lord has provided us with. Here's what the New Century Version translation says about these mighty weapons:

"We fight with weapons that are different from those the world uses. Our weapons have pow- er from God that can destroy the enemy's strong places. We destroy people's arguments." (2 Corinthians 10:4 NCV)

The goal of this book is to teach you how to use these wonderful and effective tools and weapons that God has provided to empower us and defeat the enemy!

Chapter One: The Prayer

Good morning precious Lord who art in Heaven, Hallow be thy name, thy Kingdom come, thy will be done on earth, as it is in heaven. Give us today, our daily bread and forgive us our trespasses as we forgive those who trespass against us. And lead us not into temptation, but deliver us from the evil one. Father, I plead the blood of Jesus over me, my spouse, (call out spouse's name) children and grandchildren, (call each by name) all my family members and friends. Satan, I **bind** you as the **strongman** operating against me and my family and I bind you and each and every one of your demonic forces attacking me, my family, my finances, my business and cast you all into the pits of hell, in the mighty name of Jesus! Father, loose hundreds of thousands of your mighty warrior angels to descend upon the earth realm and encamp themselves around us and keep us from the evil one. Father, let favor go before us, let each and every one of us return from home and back without any problems, hassles or delays.

Lord, order our steps today, and bless us with wisdom to hear your voice and do what you tell us to do. Holy Spirit, place a guard over our mouths and a bridle over our tongues. Father, let us decrease so you can increase in our lives. Allow those we come into contact with today, see you and not us. Let us be a blessing to somebody today, Lord. Thank you for blessing us indeed, and enlarging our territories, and that your hand is with us and that you keep us from the evil one, and we don't cause anyone any pain.

Father, this we pray, in Jesus name, and we believe we have received it now, thank you Lord, Amen.

Chapter Two: Why it works

Let's take a look at the prayer so we can see how it works to protect and bless your family. When you pray according to the Word of God, you can always count on your prayers being answered. God's word never comes back void, and once His words leave a believer's mouth, it **has to go** out and accomplish what you told it to do! Once I grasped this revelation, I put it to the test many times, and I've seen lots and lots of confessions I've spoken out loud come to pass!

In each of the following chapters, we're going to break the prayer down line by line to show you how it matches up with God's word, so you can be confident that what you're praying for will come to pass, because God said it would!

To get started, find a nice quiet place where you can be alone for thirty to sixty minutes.

Have your Bible, notebook and pen close by. Be prepared to jot down notes as you read the scriptures associated with the prayer. You always want to make sure anything pertaining to the Word of God lines up with the Word of God.

Prepare the names of the family members and friends that you would like to intercede and pray for so you can insert their names at the appro- priate time. After you become comfortable with the prayer itself, feel free to expand on it by praying for people you don't know. For instance, I have a heart for children, so I've expanded this praying by inter-ceding and standing in the gap for each and every child in the earth realm, covering them with the blood of Jesus, binding the enemy from operating in their lives and releasing God's warrior angels to en-camp themselves around each child and keep them from harm.

Once you say the prayer, sit still and wait to hear from God. He may speak to you or flood your mind with ideas and images. Jot this information down immediately. You never know what million dollar idea, invention or best selling plot line God is going to download from His Spirit to your Spirit!

In the last chapter of the book, I challenge each and every one of you to say the prayer every day for 30 days and let me know how it's affecting your life. You'll read more about this in Chapter Ten.

Chapter Three: Jesus' Perfect Prayer

"My Father, who art in Heaven, hallow be thy name, thy Kingdom come, thy will be done on earth as it is in heaven. Give us today, our daily bread and forgive us our trespasses as we forgive those who trespass against us. And lead us not into temptation, but deliver us from the evil one." (Matt. 6:9)

My Father, who art in Heaven, hallow be thy name: In Matthew 6:9 Jesus taught the disciples how to pray the perfect prayer by coming boldly to the throne of grace and addressing God as Our Father, who art in Heaven. Always enter into our Father's gates with praise and worship. Let Him know you honor him by submitting to his sovereignty in our lives by paying homage to where he lives, in heaven. Hallowed be thy name. The word hallowed means sanctified or set apart. We praise His name above all names.

Thy Kingdom come, thy will be done on earth as it is in heaven: In this part, we pray for the Kingdom of God to come and that God's will be done down here in the Earth realm as It is up in heaven. In heaven, life is wonderful. From the accounts I've read, Eden or Paradise is there. It wasn't destroyed after Adam and Eve left. It's in heaven, waiting for us to enjoy! If we could get more saints earnestly getting down on there knees and praying for God's will to be done down here on Earth as it is in heaven, imagine how much better our lives would be? God's word tells us to do just that in 2 Chronicles 7:14: "if my people, who are called by my name, will humble themselves and pray and seek my face and turn from their wicked ways, then I will hear from heaven, and I will forgive their sin and will heal their land." (NIV)

Did you see that? He will heal our land!!

Give us today, our daily bread: Our Father in Heaven expects us to rely on Him for our provision. I know that sounds crazy and ridiculous, however, with this ongoing recession we've seen what happens when we rely on man to supply our needs! Employers are making it clearer and clearer that they are more concerned about profits than people, so it's time to learn how to trust God so you can rely on Him to take care of you. This is also found in his Word. Here's the Message translation of what Jesus told the disciples in Matthew 6:25-26: "If you decide for God, living a life of God-worship, it follows that you don't fuss about what's on the table at mealtimes or whether the clothes in your closet are in fashion. There is far more to your life than the food you put in your stomach, more to your outer appearance than the clothes you hang on your body. Look at the birds, free and unfettered, not tied down to a job description, careless in the care of God. And you count far more to him than birds."

Because I rely on Him and not my salary from my full time job, I own this publishing company. This is my third book, and I'm currently conducting a five part workshop at my local library teaching other au- thors how to promote their books. I have a success- ful podcast on blogtalkradio.com called Author Chat with Lynda D. Brown, with an accompanying web-site, http://www.authorchat.info. The Lord has bless-ed me because I believed and relied on his promises to bless the works of my hands: "For the Lord your God will bless you in all your harvest and in all the work of your hands and your joy will be complete." (Deuteronomy 16:15 NIV)

My income streams have begun to flow, which helps supplement my pay check, and I can write and publish my books and maintain my website and pod-cast right from home.

Because I honor my beloved Father every morning by relying on Him, he opens the windows of heaven and blesses me even more!

Forgive us our trespasses as we forgive those who trespass against us: I can't stress the importance of this next section enough. If you have anyone that you need to forgive, this section takes care of it for you. As we forgive those who trespass against us guarantees God will hear your prayer. If you don't forgive, God won't forgive you and your prayers will not reach heaven. In verse fourteen of Matthew 6, Jesus says this: " For if you forgive other people when they sin against you, your heavenly Father will also forgive you. But if you do not forgive others their sins, your Father will not forgive your sins."(NIV)

If you're not sure that you've forgiven every-one, ask the Holy Spirit to reveal them to you.

And lead us not into temptation, but deliver us from the evil one: We pray here for God to protect us from things that may tempt us, and are harmful to us. The second section, **but deliver us from the evil one**, lines up with this scripture found in James 4:7 in the New Testament: "Submit yourselves to God, resist the devil and he will flee from you." (NIV)

Begin your prayer by praising and worshiping God with the perfect prayer and the Lord will hear your petitions.

Chapter Four: Pleading the blood of Jesus

"Father, I plead the blood of Jesus over me, my spouse, (call out spouse's name) children and grandchildren, (call each by name) all my family members and friends."

Nothing keeps the enemy away like the blood of the lamb! (Jesus)

Pleading the blood is a very powerful spiritual warfare tool that will defeat the enemy each and every time! When God instructed the Israelites to paint their doors with the blood of a lamb so the angel of death would pass them by, they did and all of the Israeli children lived, while the angel of death killed each first-born child of the Egyptian people. "By faith he kept the Passover and the application of blood, so that the destroyer of the firstborn would not touch the firstborn of Israel." (Hebrews 11:28)

God's word does not change nor does it become ineffective; it still works today. I plead the blood over my family, friends, job, national and local leaders, my finances, my publishing company, my bank accounts, the gifted contractors that assist me in the publishing of my books, etc. anything I deem important, or that God asks me to plead the blood over, I do. And it has never failed me. I can't stress the importance of this enough.

If you don't understand **pleading the blood,** and would like more information, Amazon has some wonderful books by some of the leading men and women in this revelation.
You can find a list by clicking on the resource links at the end of this book.

Speak out loud your name, your husband or wife's name, your children's names, and any family and friend that you may be concerned about. This is a great intercessory prayer, so if you have loved ones that don't have a relationship with Jesus, make sure you say their names each time you pray until you see a breakthrough!

Chapter Five: Binding the strongman

"Satan, I bind you as the strongman operating against me and my family and I bind each and every one of your demonic forces attacking me, my family, my finances, my business and cast you all into the pits of hell, in the mighty name of Jesus! Father, loose hundreds of thousands of your mighty warrior angels to descend upon the earth realm and encamp themselves around us and keep us from the evil one."

The strongman is Satan and here's the scriptural reference to prove this: "If a house is divided against itself, that house cannot stand. And if Satan opposes himself and is divided, he cannot stand; his end has come. In fact, no one can enter a strong man's house without first tying him up. Then he can plunder the strong man's house." (Mark 3:25-27 NIV)

In order to stop demonic activity in your life, you have to bind the strongman. Remember that God shared with us the keys of the kingdom, and binding Satan and his demonic forces is what we are called to do. I don't care what anyone tells you, once again, let's refer back to the Word. In Luke 9: 1-2: "Then he called his twelve disciples together, and gave them power and authority over all devils, and to cure diseases. And he sent them to preach the kingdom of God, and to heal the sick."

Just to be clear that Jesus expected the same out of

us, this is what it states in John 14:12, "Very truly I tell you, whoever believes in me will do the works I have been doing, and they will do even greater things than these, because I am going to the Father."

Binding and loosing is a major weapon that we should always keep in our spiritual arsenal! In Matthew 16:19 Jesus says, "I will give you the keys of the Kingdom of heaven; whatever you bind on earth will be bound in heaven, and whatever you loose on earth, will be loosed in heaven."

It's time for the citizens of the Kingdom of God to take control of this earth realm and start binding some of the demonic activity that's taking place here on earth. Once we bind the strongman, we can cast him and his demonic forces back to the pits of hell, in Jesus' name. **This part is very important. Please do not try to bind demons without using the name of Jesus.** The demons will not listen to you. However, they are programmed to bow down to the name of Jesus Christ, and are obligated to do what you command them to do!

Loose hundreds of thousands of your mighty warrior angels: In Psalms 91:11 it says "For he will command his angels concerning you to guard you in all your ways, they will lift you up in their hands so that you will not strike your foot against a stone."

The word angel comes from the Greek word aggelos, which means messenger. In the Bible, God always sent angels to deliver messages for him to mankind. We all know the story about Him sending Gabriel to the Virgin Mary to tell her that God intended to use her to bring forth His son Jesus. In Luke 1:12 an angel visited Zechariah and told him God was blessing him and his wife Elizabeth with a son. And last but certainly not least, the two angels who came to Earth in the form of man and warned Lot to get his family and leave Sodom and Gomorrah before the Lord destroyed it!

In this part of the prayer, we ask God's mighty warrior angels to surround us and protect us. God made the angels to help us, start using them!

Chapter Six: God's Favor, wisdom and guidance

"Father, let favor go before us. Order our steps today, Holy Spirit, place a guard over our mouth and a bridle over our tongues."

This section covers favor and allowing the Holy Spirit to order our steps and control our mouths. Let's start by looking at God's promise to bless us with his favor in Deuteronomy 28 verses 1-14 from the Message Bible. I want you to be very clear that God's promises are for us:

"If you listen obediently to the Voice of GOD, your God, and heartily obey all his commandments that I command you today, GOD, your God, will place you on high, high above all the nations of the world. All these blessings will come down on you and spread out beyond you because you have responded to the Voice of GOD, your God:

GOD's blessing inside the city
GOD's blessing in the country
GOD's blessing on your children
the crops of your land
the young of your livestock
the calves of your herds the
lambs of your flocks
GOD's blessing on your basket and bread bowl
GOD's blessing in your coming in
GOD's blessing in your going out

GOD will defeat your enemies who attack you. They'll come at you on one road and run away on seven roads.
GOD will order a blessing on your barns and workplaces; he'll bless you in the land that GOD, your God, is giving you.
GOD will form you as a people holy to him, just as he promised you, if you keep the commandments of GOD, your God, and live the way he has shown you.
All the peoples on Earth will see you living under the Name of GOD and hold you in respectful awe.
GOD will lavish you with good things: children from your womb, offspring from your animals, and crops from your land, the land that GOD promised your ancestors that he would give you. GOD will throw open the doors of his sky vaults and pour rain on your land on schedule and bless the work you take in hand. You will lend too many nations but you yourself won't have to take out a loan. GOD will make you the head, not the tail; you'll always be the top dog, never the bottom dog, as you obediently listen to and diligently keep the commands of GOD, your God, that I am command-ing you today. Don't swerve an inch to the right or left from the words that I command you today by going off following and worshiping other gods."

Aren't these some awesome promises? Just by obeying God and following His command-ments, we can eat from the good of the land!

Order our steps: In Psalms 37:23 in the King James Version, it states, "The steps of a good man are ordered by the Lord, and He delights in his ways." It goes on to say in verse 24 "that if the good man falls down, the Lord upholds him with His hands." In other words, if we stumble and fall in our walk with the Lord, He will catch us, or as the Message Bible states, "if he stumbles, he's not down for long; God has a grip on his hands." Now how great is that, knowing that God truly has our backs?

Holy Spirit put a guard over my mouth and a bridle over my tongue: This portion of the prayer reminds us about asking the Holy Spirit, our comforter, to help us: "But the Advocate, the Holy Spirit, whom the Father will send in my name, will teach you all things and will remind you of everything I have said to you." When you embrace the ministry of the Holy Spirit, the Lord can open doors of opportunity for you that you've never imagined!

Too bad that not enough teaching is done on the Holy Spirit, and people fall short by relying on themselves instead of the power that Jesus left here on Earth to assist us. The scripture reference about putting a guard over your mouth is found in Psalm 141:3 "Set a guard over my mouth, LORD; keep watch over the door of my lips." (NIV) This speaks to the reference James made in the New Testament: "A word out of your mouth may seem of no account, but it can accomplish nearly anything—or destroy it!"

"It only takes a spark, remember, to set off a forest fire. A careless or wrongly placed word out of your mouth can do that. By our speech we can ruin the world, turn harmony to chaos, throw mud on a reputation, send the whole world up in smoke and go up in smoke with it, smoke right from the pit of hell."

"This is scary: You can tame a tiger, but you can't tame a tongue—it's never been done. The tongue runs wild, a wanton killer. With our tongues we bless God our Father; with the same tongues we curse the very men and women he made in his image. Curses and blessings out of the same mouth!" (James 3:5-12MSG)

Unfortunately, too many Christians ignore this scripture. As stated in Proverb 18:21 from the King James Version, "Death and life are in the power of the tongue, and those who love it will eat its fruit." I prefer the Message version: "Words kill, words give life: they're either poison or fruit-you choose."

Wow that's powerful. You really have to start paying attention to the words that are coming out of your mouth!

Chapter Seven: Allowing God to increase in our lives

"Father, let us decrease so you can increase in our lives."

When I think of decreasing and letting God increase in my life, I use the Apostle Paul's letter to the Galatians. In Chapter five beginning with verse thirteen, Paul cautions the church to walk in the Spirit of the Lord and not in the flesh. What he meant was to allow the fruit of the Spirit to dominate your thoughts and actions. I'm going to be honest and say this is hard for those of us who are use to being in control of our lives and our families. To surrender that kind of power is essential for our growth as in- formed Christians. To walk in the flesh can be messy and destructive because according to Paul, the flesh is in conflict with the Spirit. You are not to do whatever you want! Look what Paul says in Galatians 5: 19-21 from the NIV translation about the characteristic of a Christian walking in the flesh: "The acts of the flesh are obvious: sexual immorality, impurity and debauchery; idolatry and witchcraft; hatred, discord, jealousy, fits of rage, selfish ambition, dissensions, factions , envy; drunkenness, orgies, and the like. I warn you, as I did before, that those who live like this will not inherit the kingdom of God."

Now let's look at how walking in the Spirit will enhance the life of a believer according to Gal. 5:22 from the NIV version: "But the fruit of the Spirit is love, joy, peace, forbearance, kindness, goodness, faithfulness, gentleness, and self control." And in verses 24-26, Paul reminds us that: "Those who belong to Christ Jesus have crucified the flesh with its passion and desires. Since we live by the Spirit, let us keep in step with Spirit. Let us not become conceited, provoking and envying each other."

How many Christians do you know that are walking in hatred, jealousy, envy, sexual immoral- ity, idolatry (love of money which is the spirit of mammon)? How many are into witchcraft (reading horoscopes, going to fortune tellers, palm readers, numerologists)?

In order for us to really see God move in our lives, it's imperative that we begin to train ourselves to walk in the fruit of the Spirit, so that unbelievers can see God in us. Then we'll be in a position to be a blessing to others!

Chapter Eight: More Blessings and Increase

"Thank you for blessing us indeed, and for enlarging our territory, and that your hand is with us and that you keep us from the evil one, and we don't cause anyone any pain."

In the Old Testament in 1 Chronicles, we meet a man by the name of Jabez from the tribe of Judah. In chapter four, it states that Jabez was a better man than his brothers, a man of honor. His mother had named him Jabez, which meant "pain," saying, "I bore him in pain." However, since Jabez loved the Lord and apparently followed and obeyed God's commandments, it states that when he cried out to the God of Israel ("Oh that you would bless me and enlarge my territory! Let your hand be with me, and keep me from harm so that I will be free from pain."), God granted his request!

Let's look at the prayer and see if we can figure out why God answered Jabez's prayers. Notice how it starts out that Jabez cried out to the Lord, and asked Him to bless him and enlarge his territory. God loves it when we cry out to Him for help instead of trying to do it ourselves. Like I said before, I've learned to trust his timing. I can see where God wants to take me. Being human, I'm impatient and want what I see now, but God knows when I need to slow down and wait on Him.

You may remember a book written by Dr. Bruce Wilkinson a few years ago titled, The Prayer of Jabez. I purchased a copy, said it a few times and forgot about it. In January 2011, God put it on my heart to begin saying the prayer everyday. Trusting and believing Him, I did and slowly miracles began happening in my life and my business (one of my territories).

Here are some of the things I've been blessed with since January 2011: Several copies of my first novel, published under my label, Spoken Word Press, were purchased by my local library and patrons really embraced it. When the sequel came out in August, they purchased several copies of this one as well.

In April of 2012, I listened to a sermon preached by Dr. Bill Winston. He preached about asking God to download from His Spirit to your spirit what you wanted God to do for you. Being a doer of the Word, I took up the challenge and before I went to sleep that night, I asked God, in Jesus' name, to download from His Spirit to mine how to get my Invisible En- emies Series on Amazon's best sellers list., I woke up the next morning, and all I could think about was Amazon's KDP Select program for independent pub- lishers. I'm already a member of KDP, but I had been hesitating to test the Select option that required you to sell your electronic formats strictly on Ama- zon for 90 days. But like Simon Peter, I told God the next morning when I realized where He was leading me that I had checked them out already, but at His word I would check it out again. I quickly researched authors who had used this method and had good results, and I decided to go for it.

That Saturday I registered book one under the Select option and put the book on Amazon for free for 4 days. By Wednesday, book one was off of the free list, but it was now listed at #48 in paid fiction on the best sellers list!

Wow, right in front of me was proof that God's word works. Sales for book two automatically took off and eventually both books were on the best sell- ers list for a couple of months. It was great. My third income stream began to pick up steam as authors began to sign up for my promotional package to showcase their books on my podcast, Author Chat on blogtalkradio.com.

Currently, I'm doing a five month workshop at a local library teaching authors how to promote their books. Some of you may say this is just a coinci- dence, but I tried to set up this workshop on my own, a year before to no avail. I've learned to trust God's timing and not mine and because I trust Him, He's enlarging my territory, big time!

"That your hand is with us and you keep us from the evil one and we don't cause anyone any pain."

Jabez invited God to be a part of his blessing, because he knew that if God was with him, He would keep the evil one away. The evil one comes to kill, steal and destroy.

Have you invited God to be a part of what- ever you're praying about? If not, try it, and you'll be amazed at the results.

Chapter Nine: Believe and Receive

"Father, this we pray, in Jesus name, and we believe we have received it now, thank you Lord, Amen." (Mark 11)

We believe we have received it now: It breaks my heart to know that so many Christians wait years and years for the promises of God to be fulfilled in their lives. They attend church regularly, pay tithes, are good citizens, etc. So why aren't prayers being answered?

It may surprise you to know that many Christians can't receive the promises of God, because in their hearts they really don't believe the Word of God. Oh, they say all the right religious things when they are around church folk, but once Sunday is over, they go back to their everyday lives, trying to do everything in their own power, instead of asking God for help.

I had a conversation with some female friends not too long ago, and several of the ladies, including myself, are divorced. I mentioned that I'm content to wait on God to bless me with the right man this time around. The women looked at me like I was crazy.

"Surely you don't really believe that do you, Lynda?" One of the ladies asked me.

I looked at her and smiled. "I'm tired of dealing with the wrong guys, so I will trust God to bless me with the right man, and I don't care how long it takes."

They shook their heads and looked at me with pity. "We'll I can't wait on God," one of them said, "He might take too long!"

I shook my head at all the unbelief. All of us were raised in the church and still attend regularly. But they don't believe the Word of God.

God knows your heart. You can't fool him. If you don't believe His Word, His Word can't work for you. It's that simple. One of the main culprits is the almighty tongue that we asked the Holy Spirit to guard earli- er. He's the only one strong enough to help us speak life, and not death, into our life and into the lives of others.

How many saints do you know that sit an hour or more in church, and as soon as they leave, have a shouting match with the kids in the car, spewing words that they wouldn't have dared said just min- utes before? What about a husband and wife, who have a disagreement in the car right after praying for God to heal their marriage?

Part of the problem is simply bad teaching. Too many pastors and ministers have become lazy and unpre- pared to deal with the issues of today's generation. They rely on tradition and religious ideologies to lead the church, and seem unaware or unconcerned about the welfare of their congregation. Too many Christians are being left behind in churches. However, God is still going to hold each Christian accountable to His Word, so purchase a good Bible with either a NIV (New International Version) or MSG (Message) translation that you can understand and get busy studying what God's Word says about you and what He has for you. If you read it, trust it, believe it, and act on it, your life will never be the same!

Chapter Ten: The 30-Day Challenge

''Thank you so much for purchasing this book. I pray that it is a blessing to you and your family. As I mentioned earlier, I say this prayer everyday and my immediate family is doing great. Everyone is working, everyone has a roof over their heads, and everyone is healthy.

I would like to challenge you to protect and bless your family by saying this prayer for 30 days:

1) Log onto our webpage at http://www.spokenword-press.info and sign up to take the challenge. After saying the prayer for 30 days, log onto the website and leave a testimony!

2) Keep a daily journal for the following:
   a) List Family members and friends that you're praying for.
   b) List the blessings that you're asking God for.
   c) Start teaching your children this prayer for gen erational blessings.

Bless you...

Lynda D. Brown
Author of the best selling Invisible Enemies Series

Resources:

Dr. Bill Winston: Transform Your Thinking, Transform Your Life.
http://www.amazon.com/Transform-Your-Thinking-Life-ebook/dp/B003RWSEN8/

Joyce Meyer: Change Your Words Change Your Life
http://www.amazon.com/Secret-Power-Speaking-Gods-ebook/dp/B001E2NXAC

Joyce Meyer: Filled with the Spirit: Understanding God' Power in Your Life.
http://www.amazon.com/Filled-Spirit-Understanding-Power-ebook/dp/B001J2UVRA/

Kenneth Copeland: The Blessing of the Lord makes Rich and He Adds No Sorrow with It.
http://www.amazon.com/BLESSING-Makes-Sorrow-Proverbs-ebook/dp/B005A90RFE/

Dr. Jesse Duplantis: Distortion: The Vanity of Genetically Altered Christianity.
http://www.amazon.com/Distortion-Genetically-Altered-Christianity-ebook/dp/B008RBGVUC/

Jerry Savelle: The Favor of God: Embrace All God Has Prepared for You
http://www.amazon.com/Favor-God-Embrace-Prepared-ebook/dp/B009GKRK9O/

Chip Ingram: The Invisible War, What Every Believer Needs to Know about Satan, Demons, and Spiritual Warfare
http://www.amazon.com/Favor-God-Embrace-Prepared-ebook/dp/B009GKRK9O/

Lynda D. Brown: Invisible Enemies Book One of the Invisible Enemies Series
http://www.amazon.com/Invisible-Enemies-ebook/dp/B0043M4SLS/

Lynda D. Brown: Seed of Satan: Leah's Story Book Two of the Invisible Enemies Series
http://www.amazon.com/Seed-Satan-Invisible-Enemies-ebook/dp/B005JC5Y64/

Author Biography

After publishing her first non fiction title, Once I Was Lost, with a traditional publisher in 2006, author Lynda D. Brown decided to create her own independent publishing company and Spoken Word Press was born. In May 2010, Lynda published her first novel, Invisible Enemies, a supernatural thriller with a biblical message. While writing book one, her characters began to take on lives of their own, and Lynda decided to create a series based on the characters in the original book.

In August 2011, Seed of Satan: Leah's Story, book two in the series was published,

In late October of 2010, Lynda created The Author Chat Show, an online podcast for self published authors to showcase their work. Currently the website has over one hundred and sixty members.

April 2012, Invisible Enemies and Seed of Satan were both on Amazon's Best Sellers List for a couple of months.

www.ingramcontent.com/pod-product-compliance
Lightning Source LLC
La Vergne TN
LVHW051713080426
835511LV00017B/2884